The **Lunchbox** Book

Penny Stanway

Sara Lewis

hamlyn

First published in Great Britain in 2001 by
Hamlyn, a division of Octopus Publishing Group Ltd
2–4 Heron Quays, London E14 4JP

This paperback edition first published 2003

ISBN 0 600 60786 0

A CIP catalogue record for this book
is available from the British Library

Printed and bound in China

10 9 8 7 6 5 4 3 2 1

The material in this book has also appeared
in the following Hamlyn publications:
Good Food for Kids
Veggie Food for Kids

NOTES

◎ **V** suitable for **vegetarians**

◎ All recipes are provided with **serves** information which will depend on the age and appetite of family members.

◎ Standard level **spoon measures** are used in all recipes.
1 tablespoon = one 15 ml spoon
1 teaspoon = one 5 ml spoon

◎ Both metric and imperial **measurements** are given for the recipes. Use one set of measures only, not a mixture of both.

◎ **Ovens** should be **preheated** to the specified temperature. If using a fan assisted oven, follow the manufacturer's instructions for adjusting the time and temperature. **Grills** should also be preheated.

◎ **Medium eggs** should be used unless otherwise stated.

◎ Use **full fat milk** unless otherwise specified.

◎ **Pepper** should be **freshly ground** unless otherwise stated.

◎ **Fresh herbs** should be used unless otherwise specified. If unavoidable, use dried herbs as an alternative but halve the quantities stated.

Contents

More and more **children** are choosing to take a **packed lunch** to school. In fact, 80 per cent of homes with children regularly make packed lunches. They offer a **cheaper** and often **healthier** alternative to school dinners and allow parents more **control** over what their children are eating.

The types of foods found in lunchboxes are changing; lunchboxes are no longer the preserve of the curled ham sandwich, packet of crisps and chocolate biscuit. Nowadays parents are looking to provide more interesting and diverse choices for their children. Most importantly, however, they are aiming to supply healthier food. Fresh fruits and pasta salads are on the menu, for example, along with a range of attractive vegetarian options that encourage children to eat more fruits and vegetables.

Choosing a **lunchbox**

When choosing a lunchbox think carefully about its size. It needs to be big enough to contain a decent lunch, but not so large that the food rattles around and your child carries an unnecessarily large box. Make sure the box is airtight, to keep the food fresh, and leak-proof to avoid messy spills. It is also a good idea to get a box with separate compartments or a number of smaller boxes that fit inside – this will keep different foods separate and avoid an unappetizing mess when the box is opened.

Choose an insulated box if there is no provision for keeping the boxes chilled until lunchtime, or at least one that will accommodate an ice pack. Involve your children in the selection process to make sure they are not embarrassed by their lunchboxes and will be happy to get the box out of their schoolbag at lunchtime.

A **healthy** lunch

Children need to be encouraged to eat a balanced selection of healthy foods that will fuel their whole body. A healthy packed lunch is not only enjoyable and filling but can also provide several hours of sustainable energy that will last for an afternoon of learning and play. Follow the recommendations opposite to ensure a healthy result.

- Use **organic** foods when you can as they include fewer undesirable added chemicals.

- Base your child's lunch on **starchy foods** such as bread, pasta, rice salad or potato salad to provide **energy** throughout the day.

- Include some raw **fruits** or **vegetables** for maximum benefit – avocados and citrus fruits are two good ideas.

- Any balanced meal for children should include some **protein** in the form of meat, fish, eggs, cheese or pulses.

- Include oily fish, such as smoked mackerel, sardines and poached or canned salmon, as these include useful **omega-3** fats.

- Avoid **processed** foods that may taste good but contain few **nutrients** and lots of undesirable fats, salt and sugar.

- Include a small piece of **cake** or a **biscuit** if you like, making your own from the range of healthy **recipes** in this book.

Exciting lunches

The key to keeping up your child's interest and making sure the lunches you provide are eaten every day is in the variety and imagination of the choice of foods.

Avoid giving basic sandwiches every day – try soup in a small vacuum flask, a tasty pasta salad or mini quiches or tortillas for a change. When you do make sandwiches, vary the types of bread, using fruit bread, seed bread, brown, wholemeal and white, or make filled bagels, rolls, wraps, stuffed pittas or savoury biscuits from time to time.

Sandwiches do not have to be square: try triple-deckers, Catherine wheels, diamond shapes or fingers. Many children are convinced they taste better that way.

Fresh fruits and vegetables are much more likely to be eaten if they are already peeled or cut into bite-sized pieces or sticks, especially for younger children. They are also less messy that way. Fresh fruit chunks can even be made into kebabs by threading them onto a thin length of celery stick. This makes them much more fun.

A sure-fire way to make your children look forward to opening their lunchbox is to include a surprise from time to time – just one little sweet treat will help make the whole experience one to look forward to every day.

Easy extras

Include a few items from this list to make a varied lunch:

mini box of **raisins**
dried fruits, such as apricots and dates
pumpkin seeds
popcorn
wedges of hardboiled **egg**
a small **roll** and butter
cold **sausages**
cold **chicken** pieces
a few **cheese** slices and biscuits
carrot, **celery** and **cucumber** sticks with a dip
cherry **tomatoes**
a small bunch of seedless **grapes**
apple wedges tossed in lemon juice
mini **bananas**
a peeled **satsuma**, tangerine or clementine
peeled and sliced **kiwi** fruit
a few sticks of **salami** or **ham**
fingers of **cheese**
a handful of **strawberries**
a few **plums**
celery sticks filled with cream cheese
cereal bars with fruit and nuts
yogurt or fromage frais
crisps or **poppadoms** (low-fat if possible)

Food **safety**

Schools rarely provide refrigerated places for storing lunchboxes, which can cause a problem in warm weather. Even in cold weather, lunchboxes may get stored near radiators, so it's a good idea to think carefully about what you are going to include and how it will be packed.

To keep food cool, use an insulated lunchbox when possible, or place the lunchbox in a coolbag. Slip a pre-frozen icepack into your child's lunchbox to ensure the contents remain fresh. Small ones are available for this purpose. As an alternative, freeze a carton or plastic bottle of drink overnight and place this in the lunchbox. It will have defrosted by lunchtime, but in the meantime it will keep the food cool.

Packing a lunchbox

Use greaseproof paper and kitchen foil to wrap foods and keep them moist, or place moist foods in separate small boxes within the lunchbox. Liquids such as drinks and soups can be stored in a vacuum flask to keep them hot in winter or cold in summer. Remember to include a napkin or wrapped moist wipes for sticky fingers, plus a spoon if necessary for yogurts and other desserts.

Most importantly, get the kids involved – that way they get what they want and are much more likely to eat it.

A **balanced** meal in a box

Even a single sandwich can provide a balanced meal if it is well thought-out, so there is no reason why a lunchbox cannot include everything a child needs to get through the day feeling alert and well. Use the menu suggestions below to make sure your children keep on the go all day.

Menu 1

Cheese and Oatmeal **Rolls** (page 14) filled with sliced **ham**, shredded lettuce, **tomato** and mayonnaise
small bunch of seedless **grapes**
Oat and Apple **Muffins** (page 56)
apple **juice**

Menu 2

Picnic **Pies** (page 37)
Hummus (page 38)
cucumber sticks and pitta bread for dipping
yogurt or fromage frais
slice of **malt loaf**
apple wedges tossed in lemon juice
water

Menu 3

Fruit and **Rice Salad** (page 21)
cold **sausages** or hardboiled **egg** wedges
celery and **carrot** sticks
Creamy **Raspberry Fool** (page 50)
orange juice

Variety is the key to **appetizing** sandwiches, but remember it isn't just the **flavour** of the filling that's important, but also the **texture** and **moistness**, together with the type of bread, and the sort of spread.

Bread

Vary the type of bread you use for sandwiches. Bread made from white or brown wheat flour doesn't have quite as many nutrients, or as much fibre, as bread made from wholemeal flour – which contains the whole of the grain. If a child doesn't like wholemeal, try white bread that contains added fibre. Bread made with rye or barley flour, oatmeal, or mixed grain flour is delicious for a change. Pumpernickel is often popular with children too.

Don't restrict sandwiches to sliced bread. For variety, use rolls, baps, chunks of a French stick, and mini baguettes. Pitta bread can also be split and filled. You can also sandwich fillings between wholegrain crackers or rice cakes, for a change.

Spreads

Don't always opt for butter or a similar sort of fat to spread on bread. Use your imagination and choose an original spread that complements the flavour of the filling.

- ◎ **Avocado**, mashed with lemon juice to prevent discolouring
- ◎ Cream **cheese** or curd cheese
- ◎ **Fromage frais**
- ◎ **Hummus** (page 38)
- ◎ **Mayonnaise**
- ◎ Olive oil **margarine**
- ◎ Olive **tapenade**
- ◎ **Peanut** butter

Fillings

Try the following nutritious ideas (quantities are per sandwich):

- ◎ **Beetroot and cream cheese**: Mix 50 g (2 oz) of grated cooked beetroot (not in vinegar) with 1 tablespoon of cream cheese. Stir in ½–1 teaspoon of horseradish sauce if liked.
- ◎ **BLT** (bacon, lettuce, tomato): Roughly crumble 2 rashers of crisp-grilled back bacon and mix with 2 tablespoons of sliced lettuce and 1 sliced tomato.
- ◎ **Cheese and olive**: Mix 25 g (1 oz) of grated Edam cheese with 1–2 pitted and chopped green or black olives.
- ◎ **Chicken and aubergine**: Lay one slice of roast chicken over 2 roasted or grilled slices of aubergine.
- ◎ **Chicken and avocado**: Mash ⅓–½ avocado with 1 teaspoon of lemon juice. Chop 2 slices of roast chicken and mix with the avocado.
- ◎ **Cucumber and sardine**: Mash 1 canned sardine and spread on one of the bread slices. Top with cucumber slices.
- ◎ **Egg and cress or celery**: Mash 1 cooled hard-boiled egg with 2 teaspoons of mayonnaise. Stir in a little cress or finely chopped celery.
- ◎ **Orange cheese and carrot**: Mix 1 finely grated carrot with 25 g (1 oz) of Double Gloucester or Red Leicester cheese. Add a little chutney, if liked.

Food wrapped in a **parcel** always tastes twice as **delightful**, especially if the wrapping is edible. Flour **tortillas**, wheat flour 'soft wraps', and little rice flour **pancakes** all make perfect **wrappings** for savoury fillings.

Chicken fajitas filling

2 tablespoons **corn, olive** or rapeseed (canola) **oil**
½ teaspoon **cayenne** pepper
2 teaspoons **lemon juice**
6 tablespoons Greek **yogurt**
375 g (12 oz) skinless **chicken breast**, cut into strips
1 **onion**, chopped
1 **garlic clove**, crushed
2 **carrots**, finely sliced
1 **green pepper**, chopped (optional)
4–8 flour **tortillas**

1 To make the filling, in a large bowl mix 1 tablespoon of the oil with the cayenne, lemon juice and yogurt. Add the chicken and stir to coat in the mixture. Leave to marinate in a cool place for 30 minutes, if possible.

2 Heat the remaining oil in a large frying pan. Add the onion, garlic and carrots, and cook gently for 5 minutes, stirring from time to time. Add the marinated chicken and green pepper (if using), and fry gently, for 15 minutes, until the chicken is cooked through.

3 Allow the filling to cool before making the wraps. Divide the filling between the flour tortillas, placing it to one side of the centre. Wrap the unfilled half around the filling.

4 For a lunchbox, wrap in non-stick baking paper. Serve with a salad or cherry tomatoes.

serves 4-8 **preparation time** 40 minutes **cooking time** 20 minutes

Wraps are a child-friendly way of **parcelling** up vegetables and contributing towards the 5 **recommended** helpings of **vegetables** and **fruits** a day.

These are the **solution** if you suddenly discover you've **run out** of ordinary bread for lunchboxes. They are also great for an impromptu **picnic** – **quickly** baked and taken warm, loosely wrapped in foil.

200 g (7 oz) self-raising white **flour**
2 teaspoons **baking powder**
125 g (4 oz) medium **oatmeal**
50 g (2 oz) mature vegetarian **Cheddar cheese**, grated
2 teaspoons Dijon **mustard**
4 tablespoons **olive oil**
1 **egg**, lightly beaten
5–6 tablespoons **milk**

1 Sift the flour and baking powder into a bowl. Add the oatmeal and cheese and mix together.

2 Beat the mustard, oil, egg and 5 tablespoons of the milk together in another bowl, then add to the flour mixture. Mix to a fairly soft dough, using a round-bladed knife and add a little extra milk if the dough feels dry.

3 Turn out the dough onto a floured surface and shape into a round. Cut into 8 wedges and shape each piece into a ball.

4 Place the rolls on a lightly greased large baking sheet, spacing them slightly apart. Score the top of each one twice, with a sharp knife. Bake in a preheated oven at 200°C (400°F) Gas Mark 6 for about 20 minutes until risen and golden. Transfer to a wire rack to cool before filling.

makes 8 **preparation time** 5 minutes **cooking time** 20 minutes

40 g (1½ oz) **bulgar wheat**
25 g (1 oz) frozen **broad beans**
25 g (1 oz) **green beans**, thickly sliced
2 tablespoons frozen **peas**
1 **orange**
1 **tomato**, chopped
40 g (1½ oz) canned **red kidney beans**, drained
2 teaspoons **olive oil**

(V)

1 Put the bulgar wheat into a bowl, pour on
150 ml (¼ pint) of boiling water and leave to soak for
10 minutes. Meanwhile, cook the broad beans, green
beans and peas in a small saucepan of boiling water for
3 minutes. Drain, rinse with cold water and drain again.

2 Halve the orange lengthwise and cut out the segments
from one half; squeeze the juice from the other half.

3 Drain off any excess water from the bulgar wheat, then
add the cooked vegetables, tomato, red kidney beans,
orange segments, 1 tablespoon orange juice and the oil.
Toss to mix and divide between 2 small plastic containers.
Seal well.

Make this **easy** salad the night before to **save** that early morning panic. If you are preparing only one child's packed lunch, save the other portion for your own lunch – pile it on to **salad** leaves and top with garlicky **roasted** peppers.

serves 2 **preparation time** 15 minutes **cooking time** 5 minutes

Big Bean Bonanza

This **unusual** salad with its **sweet** and **savoury** flavours keeps well in the refrigerator for a couple of days, **ready** and waiting to fill a lunchbox or make a **healthy** snack.

200 g (7 oz) **couscous**
250 ml (8 fl oz) hot fresh **vegetable stock**
2 red-skinned dessert **apples**, cored and diced
125 g (4 oz) vegetarian **Cheddar cheese**, diced
75 g (3 oz) **sultanas**
8 tablespoons **apple juice**
2 tablespoons chopped flat leaf **parsley** (optional)

▶▶ The ingredients in this salad could be **varied** to include other fruits, such as **grapes**, chopped **dried apricots** or **prunes**.

1 Put the couscous in a bowl and pour on the hot stock. Cover and leave for 15 minutes until the stock is completely absorbed. Turn the couscous into a cold bowl and fluff up the grains with a fork to separate. Leave to cool.

2 Add the diced apples, cheese, sultanas, apple juice and parsley (if using), and toss together until evenly combined. Cover and chill until required.

3 Place the salad in a well-sealed container and serve with roasted vegetables, such as aubergine slices, if you like.

serves 4-6 **preparation time** 20 minutes

If your **child** refuses to eat salad this **chunky** pasta salad might be just the recipe to convert him. **Make** it the night before and **store** in the fridge.

50 g (2 oz) small **pasta** shapes
2 tablespoons **sunflower oil**
1 teaspoon sun-dried or ordinary **tomato paste**, or ketchup
1 teaspoon wine **vinegar**
½ small **carrot**, diced
¼ red **pepper**, deseeded and diced
1 **tomato**, diced
50 g (2 oz) vegetarian **Cheddar cheese**, diced

1 Add the pasta to a saucepan of boiling water and cook until al dente – just tender.

2 Meanwhile mix the sunflower oil, tomato paste or ketchup and vinegar in a bowl until evenly blended. Add the diced carrot, red pepper, tomato and cheese; toss to mix.

3 Drain the pasta, rinse under cold running water and drain thoroughly. Add the pasta to the salad, toss together and divide between 2 small plastic containers. Seal well and pack into lunchboxes, or refrigerate if making the salad the night before.

serves 2 **preparation time** 5 minutes **cooking time** 10 minutes

The tomatoes, carrots and red peppers in this salad are all rich in beta-carotene – the brightly coloured pigment that is converted by the body into vitamin A.

There is plenty of **vitamin C** in this salad from the **kiwi**, **citrus** fruit and **orange** juice. The lentils provide **long-lasting** energy and a little **protein**.

50 g (2 oz) split **red lentils**
200 g (7 oz) long-grain **rice**
2 **mandarins**, clementines or small oranges
2 **kiwi** fruit
6 tablespoons fresh **orange juice**
2 tablespoons clear **honey** (optional)

1 Put the lentils in a small pan, cover with boiling water and cook for about 10 minutes until the lentils are tender but retaining their shape. Drain and rinse under cold running water.

2 Meanwhile, cook the rice in a separate pan until tender. Drain and rinse under cold running water; drain well.

3 Cut the skins from the oranges, removing the pith as well as the peel, then chop the flesh. Peel and chop the kiwi fruit. Blend the orange juice with the honey (if using). Combine all of the ingredients in a bowl, cover and chill until required.

This **unusual** mixture of lentils with fruit is bursting with essential **vitamins** and **nutrients** to provide your children with a **balanced** lunch. Prepare it the night before, ready to put into a tub for a packed lunch the next day.

serves 4 **preparation time** 10 minutes **cooking time** 15 minutes

Pea Soup

Soup is an ideal **nutritious** winter **warmer** for a packed lunch. Possibly not suitable for younger children, but can make a perfect **energy-giving** lunch for older children.

25 g (1 oz) **butter**
1 **onion**, chopped
1.2 litres (2 pints) fresh **chicken stock**
500 g (1 lb) shelled fresh, or frozen **peas**
small pinch of freshly grated **nutmeg**
black **pepper**
1 tablespoon **cornflour**, mixed with 2 tablespoons water
shredded fresh **mint** leaves, to garnish

1 Melt the butter in a large saucepan, add the onion and fry gently, stirring frequently, for about 5 minutes until softened but not browned. Add the stock, peas, nutmeg and pepper. Stir in the blended cornflour. Bring to the boil, partially cover and simmer for 10 minutes, stirring occasionally.

2 Let cool slightly, then purée the soup in a blender. Pour the heated soup into a thermos flask before packing in the lunchbox and accompany it with wholemeal bread, and cheese, if liked.

serves 4 **preparation time** 2-3 minutes **cooking time** 20 minutes

1 tablespoon **olive oil**
1 trimmed **leek** or onion, finely chopped
1 **garlic** clove, crushed
2 **carrots**, finely chopped
1 **celery** stick, finely chopped
750 ml (1¼ pints) **water**
50 g (2 oz) **pastina** (tiny pasta shapes)
125 g (4 oz) Savoy **cabbage**, Brussels sprouts or other
    green leafy vegetable, finely shredded
425 g (14 oz) can chopped **tomatoes**
425 g (14 oz) can flageolet or cannellini **beans**
black **pepper**
4 teaspoons chopped fresh **oregano** or basil (optional)
squeeze of **lemon juice** (optional)
salt (optional) and black **pepper**

Ⓥ

Pastina, or tiny soup pasta, comes in a **variety** of shapes. Look out for **alphabet** pasta, numerals, **dinosaurs** and space paraphernalia – **guaranteed** child appeal.

1   Heat the oil in a large saucepan. Add the leek or onion, garlic, carrots and celery and fry gently for 4 minutes. Pour in the water and bring to the boil. Add the pasta and simmer, covered, for 5 minutes.

2   Add the cabbage or other greens and simmer for a further 4 minutes. Mix in the tomatoes, beans and add pepper to taste. Stir in the herbs, lemon juice and a little salt (if using). Cook for a further 2 minutes until heated through. Serve with crusty bread, if liked, with the soup from a thermos flask.

serves 4-6 **preparation time** 10 minutes **cooking time** 15 minutes

Minestrone Soup

Chicken is always **popular**, especially when it's baked **barbecue-style**. Bake the drumsticks the day before so they are **cool** the next morning, **ready** to be packed into the lunchbox.

150 ml (¼ pint) Greek **yogurt**
2 tablespoons **redcurrant jelly**
1 tablespoon wholegrain **mustard**
1 **garlic** clove, crushed
grated rind and juice of ½ **lemon**
6–8 chicken **drumsticks**, skinned if preferred
black **pepper**

1 To make the marinade, mix the yogurt, redcurrant jelly, mustard, garlic, lemon rind and juice together in a bowl and season with pepper.

2 Add the chicken drumsticks to the bowl and, with clean hands, turn them to coat thoroughly with the mixture. Cover and leave to marinate in the refrigerator for at least 30 minutes, preferably several hours.

3 Turn the chicken and transfer to a roasting tin. Bake in a preheated oven at 190°C (375°F) Gas Mark 5 for 40–45 minutes, basting and turning halfway through cooking, until golden brown and cooked through. Allow to cool before wrapping in non-stick paper and adding to the lunchbox.

serves 3-4 **preparation time** 5 minutes **cooking time** 40-45 minutes

▸▸ A small tub of **raita** for **dipping** the drumsticks into is the **perfect** complement: mix 175 ml (6 fl oz) natural bio **yogurt** with 10 cm (4 inches) cucumber, chopped.

These little **spinach** puffs **appeal** to adults just as much as children. If you make them for a **party** set aside a few for a packed lunch the next day.

250 g (8 oz) shortcrust **pastry**
15 g (½ oz) **butter**
50 g (2 oz) **spinach**, chopped
large pinch grated **nutmeg**
50 g (2 oz) **ricotta** cheese
1 **egg** yolk
40 ml (1½ fl oz) **double** cream
black **pepper**

1 Roll out the pastry on a lightly floured work surface. Using a 6 cm (2 ½ inch) fluted cutter, cut out 24 rounds, re-rolling the trimmings as necessary. Line 24 patty tins with the pastry and prick the bases. Line with foil, fill with baking beans and bake in a preheated oven at 190°C (375°F) Gas Mark 5 for 10 minutes. Remove the foil and beans and bake for a further 5 minutes. Leave the oven on.

2 Meanwhile, melt the butter in a saucepan, add the spinach and cook until it begins to wilt. Remove the spinach from the heat, drain in a colander and season with nutmeg. Beat this into the ricotta cheese with the egg yolk, cream and pepper.

3 Arrange the baked pastry cases on baking sheets and spoon in the spinach mixture. Bake in the oven for 15 minutes. Allow to cool completely before serving.

makes 24 **preparation time** 20 minutes **cooking time** 30 minutes

1 teaspoon sunflower **oil**
50 g (2 oz) cooked **potato**, diced
2.5 cm (1 inch) piece **courgette**, diced
1 button **mushroom**, sliced
1 slice of **onion**, finely chopped
½ **garlic** clove, crushed (optional)
1 free-range **egg**
salt and black **pepper** (optional)

1 Heat the oil in a small 11 cm (4½ inch) nonstick frying pan (see below) and add the potatoes, vegetables and garlic, if using. Fry, stirring, for 4–5 minutes until the potatoes are lightly browned.

2 Beat the egg in a bowl with a little seasoning if required, then pour over the vegetables in the pan. Fry over a medium heat until the underside is browned. Place the pan under a medium grill for a few minutes until the egg on the surface is cooked and golden.

3 Allow the tortilla to cool, then cut in half and wrap in foil before packing in a lunchbox.

Cook an **extra** potato when you have **supper** and use it to make this easy Spanish-style **omelette**. If preferred, pop the tortilla halves into a halved pitta bread with a few slices of **tomato** or a little **ketchup**.

serves 1 **preparation time** 5 minutes **cooking time** 10 minutes

Takeaway Tortilla

Traditionally made with dried **chickpeas**, these little **spicy** patties are popular with young and old alike. Here they are made with frozen broad beans for **speed**, and mixed with a little chopped **feta** for added **flavour**.

150 g (5 oz) frozen baby **broad beans**
½ small **onion**, roughly chopped
½ teaspoon ground **cumin**
1 teaspoon ground **coriander**
2 tablespoons chopped fresh **parsley** (optional)
50 g (2 oz) **feta cheese**, well drained, chopped
1 tablespoon plain **flour**
2 tablespoons sunflower **oil**
6 mini **pitta** breads
1 Little Gem **lettuce**, roughly torn
3 tablespoons natural bio **yogurt** (optional)
little finely chopped fresh **mint** (optional)
¼ **cucumber**, sliced
1 dessert **apple**, cored and sliced

1 Add the broad beans to a pan of boiling water, bring back to the boil and simmer for 4 minutes; drain.

2 Put the beans into a food processor with the onion, spices, parsley, if using, and feta. Process until finely chopped, or finely chop all the ingredients by hand and mix in a bowl.

3 Divide the mixture into 6 portions, then press into small oval patties between well floured hands. Heat the oil in a frying pan and fry the falafel for 5 minutes, turning several times until golden.

4 Split the pitta breads open, pop a little lettuce and a falafel into each one, then spoon in a little plain yogurt, or yogurt flavoured with chopped mint, if liked. Serve with cucumber and apple slices.

makes 6 **preparation time** 10 minutes **cooking time** 10 minutes

By using the **yogurt** as an accompaniment you are complementing the **flavours** of the falafel **well**; however, please note that it may make the falafel go **soft** by lunchtime.

Cheesy Vegetable Pasties

These mini pasties make **tasty** snacks or packed lunch fillers, and you can **vary** the **choice** of vegetables in the filling to suit your family's **tastes** – sweetcorn, green beans and courgettes are equally **suitable**.

▶▶ The milk, flour and carrots in these pasties provide **plenty** of **calcium** – **essential for** growing **children**, to ensure **strong bones** and teeth.

Pastry

125 g (4 oz) plain wholemeal **flour**

125 g (4 oz) plain white **flour**

150 g (5 oz) unsalted **butter**, cut into small pieces

2–3 tablespoons cold **water**

Filling

3 tablespoons olive, rapeseed (canola) or walnut **oil**

1 small **onion**, finely chopped

2 teaspoons plain **flour**

225 ml (7 fl oz) **milk**

75 g (3 oz) vegetarian **Cheddar cheese**, grated

1 medium **carrot**, grated

1 small **potato**, finely diced

125 g (4 oz) **broccoli** florets, cut into small pieces

50 g (2 oz) frozen **peas**

beaten **egg**, to glaze

1 To make the pastry, put the flours in a food processor, add the butter and process until the mixture resembles breadcrumbs. Add the water and work briefly to a smooth dough, adding a little more water if necessary. Wrap and chill.

2 Heat the oil in a saucepan. Add the onion and fry for 3 minutes. Stir in the flour, then add the milk, cheese, carrot, potato, broccoli and peas. Bring to the boil and cook for 2 minutes, stirring constantly, until the sauce has thickened. Leave to cool.

3 Divide the dough into 8 portions. Roll out each piece to a 16 cm (6½ inch) round, using a small plate as a guide. Trim the edges and brush with beaten egg. Divide the filling between the pastry rounds, placing it in the centre. Bring the edges of the pastry up over the filling and press together firmly to make pasty shapes. Crimp the edges, using your fingers.

4 Transfer to a greased baking sheet and brush with beaten egg. Bake in a preheated oven at 200°C (400°F) Gas Mark 6 for about 25 minutes until the pastry is golden. Transfer to a wire rack to cool. Allow to cool completely before packing in a lunchbox and serve with cherry tomatoes or a tomato salad if you like.

makes 8 **preparation time** 25 minutes **cooking time** 32 minutes

These **mini** tartlets will not only provide **essential** calcium and protein but can also make an **interesting** savoury **treat** for any packed lunch.

250 g (8 oz) shortcrust **pastry**
150 g (5 oz) **onion**, finely chopped
6 tablespoons **milk**
150 g (5 oz) vegetarian **Cheddar** cheese, grated
125 g (4 oz) vegetarian **Red Leicester** cheese, grated
1 **egg**, beaten
salt and black **pepper**

1 Roll out the pastry thinly on a lightly floured work surface and use to line about twenty 6 cm (2½ inch) tartlet tins. Chill for 30 minutes.

2 Put the onion and milk into a saucepan. Bring to the boil, then simmer for 1 minute. Remove from the heat and stir in the cheeses, egg and salt and pepper. Leave to stand for 5 minutes.

3 Divide the cheese mixture among the tartlets. Bake in a preheated oven at 200°C (400°F) Gas Mark 6 for 15 minutes until golden. Allow the tartlets to cool completely before serving.

makes 20 **preparation time** 15 minutes **cooking time** 15 minutes

2–3 tablespoons sunflower **oil**

50 g **hazelnuts**

25 g (1 oz) **butter** or margarine

1 small **onion**, finely chopped

150 g (5 oz) peeled, deseeded **pumpkin** (prepared weight), coarsely grated

150 g (5 oz) vegetarian **Cheddar cheese**, grated

175 g (6 oz) fresh white **breadcrumbs**

2 free–range **eggs**, separated

salt and black **pepper** (optional)

(V)

1 Heat 1 teaspoon of the oil in a frying pan, add the hazelnuts and fry for 2–3 minutes until golden, shaking the pan constantly. Remove from the pan and chop finely.

2 Heat the butter or margarine in the frying pan, add the onion and fry, stirring, for 4–5 minutes, until softened and lightly browned. Stir in the pumpkin and cook for 2 minutes. Take the pan off the heat and stir in the cheese, 75 g (3 oz) of the breadcrumbs, the egg yolks, chopped hazelnuts and a little seasoning, if liked.

3 Lightly beat the egg whites in a shallow dish with a fork. Divide the sausage mixture into 8 portions and shape into small sausages. Dip in the egg white, then roll in the remaining breadcrumbs to coat completely.

4 Heat the remaining oil in the cleaned frying pan, add the sausages and fry for 4–5 minutes, turning several times, until golden.

makes 8 **preparation time** 10 minutes **cooking time** 15 minutes

Most children love **ketchup** with sausages, but do **look** for a brand that is comparatively **low** in salt and **sugar**. Make these sausages for the **family** meal and use any leftovers for next day's packed **lunch**.

Cheesy Pumpkin Sausages

Homemade pizzas are much more **delicious** than shop-bought ones. Add your child's **favourite** foods as alternative **toppings** to this **basic** pizza recipe.

▶▶ The popular combination of tomatoes and onions in this basic pizza topping provides **valuable nutrients** that can offer some **protection** from coughs, colds and other infections.

Pizza bases

250 g (8 oz) strong plain white **flour**
250 g (8 oz) strong plain **wholemeal flour**
1 teaspoon caster **sugar**
1 sachet easy-blend active dried **yeast**
2 tablespoons **olive oil**
3 tablespoons **milk**
175 ml (6 fl oz) hand-hot **water** (approximately)

Tomato & garlic topping

2 tablespoons olive or corn **oil**
2 **garlic** cloves, crushed
500 g (1 lb) **tomatoes**, skinned if preferred, chopped
4 tablespoons **tomato paste**, preferably sun-dried (optional)
2 tablespoons chopped fresh **oregano**, or 2 teaspoons dried
12 pitted **black olives** (optional)
300 g (10 oz) **mozzarella cheese**, finely sliced
black **pepper**
2 tablespoons **extra-virgin olive oil** for sprinkling (optional)

1 To make the pizza dough, put the flours in a bowl and stir in the sugar and yeast. Make a well in the centre and add the oil, milk and water. Mix to a smooth, pliable dough that forms a ball and leaves the sides of the bowl clean – add more milk and water if needed. Knead for 5 minutes, then place in a clean bowl, cover with a tea towel and leave to rise in a warm place for 1 hour. Knead the risen dough a little to release air, then break into 4 pieces. Press into thin rounds and transfer to oiled baking sheets.

2 To make the topping, heat the oil in a large frying pan, add the garlic and fry gently for 1 minute. Add the tomatoes and fry for 3–4 minutes, stirring frequently. Season with pepper.

3 Prick the pizzabases all over with a fork, then spread a tablespoon of tomato paste evenly on each one. Divide the garlic and tomato mixture between the bases, spreading it to the edges. Leave the pizzas to stand for 20 minutes so they rise a little.

4 Bake the pizzas in the preheated oven at 200°C (400°F) Gas Mark 6 for 15 minutes. Sprinkle with oregano and the olives (if using). Lay the mozzarella slices on top and sprinkle with olive oil if required. Bake for a further 10 minutes until the cheese has melted.

makes 4 **preparation time** 15 minutes **cooking time** 30 minutes

These **tasty** pies are made in sections of a muffin tray to ensure that they are just the **right** size for a **young** child to **hold**; there is also **sufficent** depth for plenty of the quiche-style filling.

Pastry

100 g (3½ oz) plain **flour**
100 g (3½ oz) wholemeal **flour**
50 g (2 oz) block **margarine**, diced
50 g (2 oz) white vegetable
    shortening, diced
3–4 tablespoons **water**

Filling

100 g (3½ oz) vegetarian **Cheddar**
    cheese, grated
2 **tomatoes**, thinly sliced
3 free–range **eggs**
300 ml (½ pint) **milk**
salt and black **pepper**

◀◀ The wholemeal flour in these little pies will **increase** your family's **fibre** intake, which among other things is **good** for **digestion**.

1 Lightly oil 12 sections of a muffin tray. To make the pastry, put the flours into a bowl, add the fats and rub into the flour using your fingertips (or an electric mixer) until the mixture resembles fine breadcrumbs. Add enough water to mix to a smooth dough.

2 Lightly knead the dough and roll out thinly on a lightly floured surface. Stamp out 10 cm (4 inch) rounds, using a fluted cutter (or small saucer as a guide). Use to line the muffin tins, gently pressing the pastry into the edges. Re-roll the pastry trimmings and cut more rounds as needed.

3 Divide two-thirds of the cheese between the pastry cases. Add the sliced tomatoes, halving them to fit if large.

4 Beat the eggs and milk together in a bowl with a little seasoning. Pour into the tart cases and sprinkle with the remaining cheese. Bake in a preheated oven at 180°C (350°F) Gas Mark 4 for 20–25 minutes until it is the filling is set and golden.

5 Loosen the pastry edges with a small knife and leave the pies to cool in the tin. Transfer to a plastic box and store in the fridge for up to 2 days.

makes 12 **preparation time** 12 minutes **cooking time** 25 minutes

Hummus is excellent for **dipping** into at **parties**, and it's also a **popular** packed lunch item to provide in a little plastic tub. **Flavourings** can be adjusted to suit individual **tastes**.

425 g (14 oz) canned **chickpeas**, drained
3 tablespoons **tahini**
1 **garlic** clove, crushed
1 tablespoon **sesame oil**
juice of ½ **lemon**
a little **water** to mix (if required)

1 Put the chickpeas in an electric blender or a food processor with the tahini, garlic, sesame oil and lemon juice. Blend until smooth, adding a little water if necessary so the texture is easily spoonable.

2 Place in a well-sealed container and serve with pitta bread, raw carrot or celery sticks.

Alternative dips

Cream cheese and pineapple dip Mix 125 g (4 oz) cream cheese with 1 tablespoon mayonnaise and 2 peeled, cored and chopped rings of fresh pineapple (or canned in natural juice). Add 25 g (1 oz) of diced ham if you like.

Tuna Dip Blend ½ small onion, 175 g (6 oz) tuna canned in oil, 1 tablespoon fromage fraise or mayonnaise, and 1 tablespoon chopped fresh parsley.

Yogurt and date dip Mix 175 ml (6 fl oz) thick creamy yogurt with 50 g (2 oz) chopped stoned dates.

serves 4-6 **preparation time** 10 minutes

▶▶ **Sesame** seeds in the tahini offer protein, calcium, iron, and the essential **omega-6** fatty acid – linoleic acid – which is **especially** good for **skin**, **hair** and **nails**.

This **unusual** pâté has a **delicious** flavour that **appeals** to adults and children alike. Use very **fresh** chicken so that you can **store** the pâté in the fridge for a couple of days and use as required.

2 boneless, skinless **chicken breasts**
1 tablespoon olive **oil**
125 g (4 oz) **quark** or other curd cheese
400 g (13 oz) can **red kidney beans**, rinsed and drained
3 tablespoons red **pesto**
2 tablespoons **lemon juice**
salt and black **pepper**

1 Halve the chicken breasts horizontally. Line a grill rack with foil and brush with a little of the oil. Lay the chicken breasts on the foil and brush with the remaining oil. Cook under a moderate grill for about 8–10 minutes, turning once until cooked through and pale golden. Leave to cool slightly.

2 Put the chicken in a food processor and process until finely chopped. Add the curd cheese, red kidney beans, pesto, lemon juice and a little seasoning. Blend to a fairly smooth paste.

3 Transfer to a small serving container, cover and refrigerate for up to 2 days. Serve with grainy bread, or spread in mini pittas with some sliced tomato and cucumber if you like.

serves 6-8 **preparation time** 10 minutes **cooking time** 10 minutes

200 g (7 oz) cream **cheese**
300 ml (½ pint) soured **cream**
4 hard-boiled **eggs**, shelled
2 tablespoons snipped **chives**
salt and **black pepper**

Ⓥ

1 Beat the cream cheese in a bowl until softened and smooth. Gradually mix in the soured cream.

2 Cut the eggs in half. Scoop out the yolks and set aside. Finely chop the egg whites and add to the cream cheese mixture with the chives and salt and pepper to taste.

3 Spoon the dip into individual containers and sieve the egg yolk over the top.

Served with crisp **celery sticks** and some grainy bread, this **tasty** dip makes an **healthy** lunchbox recipe for children who are old enough to **manage** a dip without getting into a mess.

Cream Cheese & Egg Dip

serves 8 **preparation time** 10 minutes

Cheese straws are one of life's small **luxuries**. Apart from being an **excellent** party food, they are also good for packed lunchboxes and picnics. Straws are **quick** and **easy** but, if you have time, shape the dough into hearts, rings, or even the first letter of your child's name.

75 g (3 oz) wholemeal **flour**
50 g (2 oz) plain **flour**
100 g (3½ oz) **butter**, cut into small pieces
1 **egg**, separated
50 g (2 oz) vegetarian Cheddar, or Parmesan **cheese**, finely grated
pinch of **cayenne pepper**
½ teaspoon **mustard powder** (optional)
2 teaspoons **poppy seeds** (optional)

1 Combine the flours in a bowl and rub in the butter until the mixture resembles fine breadcrumbs. Add the egg yolk, cheese, cayenne, and mustard powder (if using). Stir with a fork, then knead lightly until smooth.

2 Roll out the cheese pastry on a floured work surface to a 5mm (¼ inch) thickness. Cut into long strips or 'straws' and brush with beaten egg white.

3 Give each strip a half-twist in the middle before laying on a lightly oiled baking tray. Sprinkle with poppy seeds (if using).

4 Bake in a preheated oven at 200°C (400°F) Gas Mark 6 for 10–12 minutes. Cool on a wire rack.

makes 30 **preparation time** 15 minutes **cooking time** 10-12 minutes

▶▶ These cheese straws will keep well in an **airtight** tin for 3 or 4 days – but if you make **double** the amount of cheese pastry, you can **freeze** half of it to roll out and cook for another occasion.

Pumpkin Seed Breadsticks

,Keep a supply of these handy in the **freezer** and take out a few at a time as you **need** them. They will **keep** for about 6 weeks, and **defrost** in about 30 minutes at room temperature, and could be **served** with carrot sticks and dips for a more **filling** snack.

4 tablespoons **pumpkin seeds**
4 tablespoons olive **oil**
750 g (1½ lb) strong white bread **flour**
7 g (¼ oz) sachet easy-blend dried **yeast**
2 tender stems of fresh **rosemary, leaves** very finely chopped
500 ml (17 fl oz) warm **water** (approximately)

1 Add the pumpkin seeds to a heated small heavy-based frying pan and toss over a medium heat for about 1 minute until lightly toasted. Grind the toasted seeds with 2 tablespoons of the oil to a smooth paste in a clean spice or coffee grinder, or using a pestle and mortar.

2 Put the flour into a bowl, add the pumpkin seed paste, yeast and rosemary, then mix in enough water to form a soft but not sticky dough. Knead vigorously on a well-floured surface, then cut the dough into 60 pieces. Roll each into a rope, about 20 cm (8 inches) long.

3 Lay the dough sticks on 2 large oiled baking trays, spacing them slightly apart. Brush lightly with the remaining oil and cover loosely with clingfilm. Leave to prove in a warm place for about 20 minutes or until well risen. Remove the clingfilm.

4 Bake the breadsticks in a preheated oven at 220°C (425°F) Gas Mark 7 for 8–10 minutes, transposing the trays after 5 minutes to ensure even cooking. Transfer to wire racks to cool. Put a few breadsticks in an airtight container and use within 24 hours. Freeze the rest.

makes 60 **preparation time** 10 minutes **cooking time** 11 minutes

1 **beetroot**
½ **sweet potato**
2 **carrots**
1 **parsnip**
½ **celeriac**
corn or rapeseed (canola) **oil** for brushing

1 Peel the vegetables and cut into wafer-thin slices, no more than 1–2 mm (¹⁄₁₆ inch) thick. Pat the slices dry between double layers of kitchen paper, then place in a single layer on 2 baking trays.

2 Brush each vegetable slice lightly, but thoroughly, with a little oil, to bring out the natural sweetness. Turn the crisps over and brush the other sides with oil.

3 Bake in a preheated oven at 200°C (400°F) Gas Mark 6 for 10–12 minutes or until golden brown and cooked through. Celeriac, sweet potato and beetroot may need a further 1–2 minutes. (Note that beetroot colours only slightly; it shouldn't brown.) Transfer the crisps to a double layer of kitchen paper and leave to cool.

4 They will crisp up more on cooling, but should be served as soon as possible thereafter, otherwise they will start to soften. Ensure they are packed in an airtight container or bag before packing in a lunchbox. These crisps are ideal for dipping into Hummus and other dips (see page 38).

This is a very **effective** way of **encouraging** children to eat **vegetables**! Choose a selection of colours from deep **pink** beetroot, to **orange** sweet potato for **optimum** child **appeal**.

serves 4-6 **preparation time** 10 minutes **cooking time** 10-12 minutes

Vegetable Crisps

These cheesy **biscuits** seem to **melt** in the mouth. Get your **small helper** to weigh out the ingredients, roll the dough and **help** with **shaping**.

75 g (3 oz) wholemeal **flour** (or white, or half wholemeal/half white flour)
75 g (3 oz) **butter** or block margarine, diced
75 g (3 oz) vegetarian **Cheddar cheese**, grated
1 free-range **egg**, separated
1 tablespoon **sesame seeds** (optional)

1 Put the flour into a bowl, add the butter and rub in using your fingertips (or a mixer) until the mixture resembles fine breadcrumbs. Stir in the cheese, then mix in the egg yolk to make a smooth dough.

2 Gently knead the dough, then roll out on a lightly floured surface to a 5 mm (¼ inch) thickness. Cut out rounds, using a 6 cm (2½ inch) plain round cutter. From these, cut noughts, using a 3 cm (1¼ inch) plain round cutter. Using a palette knife, carefully lift the noughts on to a large baking sheet.

3 Draw a broad cross on a piece of card, about 6 cm (2½ inches) high. Cut out and use as a template to cut crosses from the dough. Lift the crosses on to the baking sheet. Re-roll trimmings to cut more shapes.

4 Brush with egg white and sprinkle with sesame seeds, if using. Bake in a preheated oven at 190°C (375°F) Gas Mark 5 for 10 minutes until golden. Leave to cool on the baking sheet.

5 Store the biscuits in an airtight container and eat within 2 days.

makes 20 **preparation time** 25 minutes **cooking time** 10 minutes

These savoury **treats** are a **healthier** option than sweet biscuits – especially if served with **apple** slices and a drink of **milk**.

A fresh fruit dessert is **straightforward** to prepare, **easy** for children to eat, and always **popular**. Most fruits are **available** all year round, but it makes **sense** to choose **homegrown** varieties when they are in **season**, and at their **peak** of flavour.

▶▶ The fresh fruit in these salads is laden with **plant pigments**, **vitamin C** and other **antioxidants**, all of which help **boost immunity** and **keep** the body healthy.

2 **kiwi** fruit
2 fresh ripe **pears**
175 g (6 oz) **raspberries**
300 ml (½ pint) **fruit juice**, such as apple and pear, apple and raspberry, red grape or pineapple juice

Ⓥ

1 Carefully peel the skin away from the kiwi fruit and chop into bite-sized pieces. Core and slice the pears, ensuring they are chopped into manageable sizes.

2 Mix the raspberries, kiwi fruit and pears together in a large bowl and add the chosen fruit juice.

3 Place individual portions in air-tight containers ready to be packed into a lunchbox.

Variations

Apple and orange salad peel and segment 1 orange; squeeze the juice from another orange. Put this in a large bowl and add 1 apple, cored and chopped, 1 pear, cored and chopped, and 200 ml (7 fl oz) of apple juice. Toss to mix. Slice 1–2 bananas and add to the fruit salad just before serving otherwise the banana will discolour. Toss to mix.

Melon and blueberry salad Quarter, deseed, peel and chop 1 small melon. Toss with 175 g (6 oz) of fresh blueberries in 300 ml (½ pint) of apple juice.

serves 4-6 **preparation time** 5 minutes

Raspberries are one of life's great **treats**, with their deep rose colour and **intense flavour**. Occasionally raspberries are so **sweet** they need no extra sugar, but they usually require a little.

200 g (7 oz) fresh **raspberries**
2–3 tablespoons **icing sugar** (preferably unrefined)
5 tablespoons double **cream**
200 g (7 oz) **fromage frais**

1 Set aside 25 g (1 oz) of the raspberries. Purée the rest in a blender or food processor, then press through a sieve into a bowl to remove the seeds. Stir in the icing sugar to taste.

2 Whip the cream in a separate bowl until thickened, then fold in the fromage frais. Add the raspberry purée and beat again until smooth and slightly thickened. Taste for sweetness.

3 Spoon into single containers and chill until required. Scatter with the reserved raspberries to serve.

serves 6 **preparation time** 8-10 minutes

2 large **oranges**, freshly squeezed
125 g (4 oz) stoned **dates**
300 g (10 oz) natural bio **yogurt**
1 **banana**, sliced, to serve

Even the flavour of mild **creamy** bio yogurt can be a little too much for young children. Mix it with this naturally **sweet** date **purée** and you are sure to **win** them round.

1 Make the orange juice up to 275 ml (9 fl oz) with water and put into a small pan with the dates. Bring to the boil, cover and simmer for 10 minutes until soft. Allow to cool slightly, then purée in a food processor or blender until smooth. Set aside until completely cooled.

2 Put alternate spoonfuls of date purée and yogurt in 4 small airtight containers, then swirl together attractively, using a small knife or skewer. Chill in the refrigerator until required.

3 Top the fruit fools with sliced banana just before packing in a lunchbox.

serves 6 **preparation time** 10 minutes **cooking time** 10 minutes

Date & Orange Fool

For this **delicious** alternative to bought fruit yogurt, a **creamy** pudding made from quick-cooking **millet** flakes is mixed with **natural** bio yogurt and layered with an assortment of **fruits**.

25 g (1 oz) **millet** flakes
300 ml (½ pint) **milk**
2 **kiwi** fruit, peeled
2 ripe **peaches** or nectarines, halved and stoned
150 g (5 oz) **strawberries**
150 g (5 oz) natural bio **yogurt**
2–3 tablespoons caster **sugar** (optional)

1 Put the millet flakes and milk into a small pan and slowly bring to the boil. Simmer gently, stirring constantly, for 3–4 minutes, until thickened and creamy, rather like the consistency of porridge. Take off the heat, cover and leave to cool. Meanwhile finely chop the fruits, keeping them separate.

2 Fold the yogurt and sugar, if using, into the cooled millet mixture. Spoon the chopped kiwi fruit into the base of four 250 ml (8 fl oz) small airtight containers. Cover with half of the yogurt mixture, then the chopped peaches. Spoon the remaining yogurt mixture over the peaches and top with the strawberries.

3 Chill the sundaes in the refrigerator until ready to be packed in a lunchbox.

serves 4 **preparation time** 5 minutes **cooking time** 3-4 minutes

250 g (8 oz) white self-raising **flour**
½ teaspoon **salt**
125g (4 oz) **butter**
175 g (6 oz) caster **sugar**
125 g (4 oz) ready-to-eat dried **apricots**
50 g (2 oz) **pecan nuts**
125 g (4 oz) **sultanas**
500 g (1 lb) ripe **bananas**
2 **eggs**

1 Grease a 23 x 12 x 7 cm (9 x 5 x 3 inch) loaf tin and line with a strip of greaseproof paper cut the width of the base and long enough to overlap both ends.

2 Sift the flour and salt into a large mixing bowl. Add the butter cut into pieces to the flour and rub in with fingertips. Stir in the sugar. Snip the dried apricots into pieces. Set aside 6 pecan nuts and coarsely chop the remainder. Add the apricots, chopped pecan nuts and sultanas and mix. Peel and mash the bananas and add with the eggs – no extra liquid is required. Beat with a wooden spoon to blend the ingredients.

3 Spoon the mixture into the prepared tin and spread level. Arrange the reserved pecan nuts on top. Place in a preheated oven at 180°C (350°F) Gas Mark 4 and bake for 1–1¼ hours. Allow to cool in the tin for 20 minutes, then loosen the unlined sides and lift the banana bread out by the paper ends. Leave until completely cold.

serves 10 **preparation time** 20 minutes **cooking time** 1–1¼ hours

This **easy-to-make**, moist banana cake is made all the better by the addition of **naturally** sweet dried **apricots.** A small slice would be a perfect **sweet** treat for any lunchbox.

Banana & Apricot Bread

Cranberry Crunch

▶▶ Sunflower seeds are a good **source** of protein and **vitamin E**; they are also high in **linoleic acid** – needed for the **maintenance** of cell membranes.

4 tablespoons **sunflower seeds**
2 tablespoons sunflower **oil**
75 g (3 oz) soft **margarine**
125 g (4 oz) light muscovado **sugar**
1 free-range **egg**
100 g (3½ oz) self-raising white **flour**
75 g (3 oz) self-raising wholemeal **flour**
grated rind of ½ small **orange**
75 g (3 oz) packet dried **cranberries**

1 Dry-fry the sunflower seeds in a nonstick frying pan, stirring constantly, for 2–3 minutes until golden. Grind to a fine paste with the oil, using a spice grinder or pestle and mortar.

2 Cream the margarine and sugar together in a bowl (or food processor). Gradually beat in the egg, then mix in the flours. Mix in the sunflower paste, then stir in the orange rind and cranberries.

3 Drop heaped teaspoonfuls of the mixture on to lightly oiled baking sheets, spacing well apart. Bake in a preheated oven at 180°C (350°F) Gas Mark 4 for 10 minutes until golden. Leave on the baking sheets to firm up for a few minutes, then transfer to a wire rack to cool.

There is something

irresistible about

the wonderful **aroma**

of **freshly** baked

biscuits. Although they

can be kept in an

airtight tin for 2–3

days, most of these

will **disappear** before

they even have a

chance to go cold!

makes about 25 **preparation time** 5 minutes **cooking time** 12-13 minutes

Muffins are one of the **easiest** cakes to make and they are **perfect** for lunchbox fillers. Muffins are best eaten **fresh** within 24 hours of baking, or frozen on the day they are made.

125 g (4 oz) plain white **flour**
125 g (4 oz) wholemeal plain **flour**
1 tablespoon **baking powder**
50 g (2 oz) medium **oatmeal**
50 g (2 oz) light muscovado **sugar**
3 small dessert **apples**, peeled, cored and diced
50 g (2 oz) **sultanas** or raisins
50 g (2 oz) unsalted **butter**, melted and cooled slightly
150 ml (¼ pint) **yogurt**
150 ml (¼ pint) **milk**
1 **egg**
5 tablespoons clear **honey**
a little extra **oatmeal**, for dusting

1 Line a 12-hole muffin tray or deep bun tray with paper muffin cases. Mix the flours, baking powder, oatmeal and sugar in a bowl. Stir in the chopped apples and sultanas or raisins.

2 In another bowl, beat together the butter, yogurt, milk, egg and honey. Add this mixture to the dry ingredients and stir quickly and briefly, until just incorporated; do not over-mix.

3 Divide the mixture between the paper cases and sprinkle with a little extra oatmeal. Bake in a preheated oven at 200°C (400°F) Gas Mark 6 for 18–20 minutes until just firm to the touch. Transfer to a wire rack to cool.

makes 12 **preparation time** 10 minutes **cooking time** 18-20 minutes

▶▶ Oatmeal is a **'low-GI food'**; this means it provides **long-lasting** energy that will **help** keep your children going without flagging during the afternoon.

A subtle way to

encourage reluctant

fruit eaters, these

deliciously **moist**

muffins are made with

naturally sweet fruit

so there's no need to

add extra sugar.

200 g (7 oz) self-raising **flour**
½ teaspoon **baking powder**
2 free-range **eggs**, beaten
5 tablespoons sunflower **oil**
5 tablespoons **milk**
1 teaspoon **vanilla essence**
2 ripe **bananas**, about 325 g (11 oz) unpeeled weight
100 g (3½ oz) **milk chocolate chips**

1 Line a 12-hole muffin tray with paper muffin cases. Sift the flour and baking powder together into a mixing bowl. Beat the eggs, oil, milk and vanilla essence together in a separate bowl.

2 Mash the bananas on a plate, using a fork, then add to the flour with the egg mixture and fork the ingredients together briefly until only just mixed. Stir in the chocolate chips.

3 Spoon into the paper cases and bake in a preheated oven at 200°C (400°F) Gas Mark 6 for 15 minutes until the muffins are well risen and the tops spring back when lightly pressed with the fingertips.

4 Transfer to a wire rack to cool. Store in an airtight container for up to 2 days or freeze on the day they are made.

makes 12 **preparation time** 10 minutes **cooking time** 15 minutes

▶▶ These muffins are bursting with **bananas** and **chocolate** – both ideal for supplying **energy** throughout the day.

◀◀ The oats and dried fruit in these flapjacks are **rich** in **fibre**. Oats in particular are **especially** rich in **soluble** fibre – the sort that helps keep **blood-sugar** levels steady and **energy** from flagging.

50 g (2 oz) **butter**

75 g (3 oz) muscovado **sugar**

1 teaspoon powdered **ginger** (optional)

4 tablespoons **rapeseed** (canola) oil

250 g (8 oz) **rolled oats**

24 g (1 oz) **sultanas**

50 g (2 oz) chopped **apricots**, papaya, pears or peaches (or a mixture)

Flapjacks are always **popular** and this version with its hint of **ginger** and moist, **chewy** dried fruit is especially good. You can omit the ginger if you like, though it does give a warm, mildly **spicy** flavour.

1 Line a 30 x 20 cm (12 x 8 inch) Swiss roll tin with non-stick baking paper. Put the butter and sugar in a large saucepan and heat gently until melted, then stir in the ginger (if using) and oil. Add the oats, sultanas and fruit, and stir to mix.

2 Spoon the mixture into the preheated tin, level the surface and press down gently. Bake in a preheated oven at 180°C (350°F) Gas Mark 4 for 35 minutes. Leave in the tin for 10 minutes, then cut into slices. Leave until cold before removing from the tin.

3 Serve the flapjacks on their own, or accompanied with a small tub of stewed apple or plums as a dessert.

makes 20 **preparation time** 5 minutes **cooking time** 35 minutes

61

One way of ensuring that your children eat enough **vegetables** and **fruit** is to incorporate them into as many recipes as you can. Top these deliciously moist cakes with a cream cheese **frosting** for extra **appeal**.

▶▶ By using rapeseed (canola) oil in these cup cakes you are **eliminating** the **saturated fat** that would be provided by using butter, making it an **healthier** sweet treat.

175 g (6 oz) self-raising wholemeal **flour**
125 g (4 oz) muscovado **sugar**
2 teaspoons **baking powder**
1 teaspoon ground **cinnamon**
pinch of ground **nutmeg**
3 free-range **eggs**, beaten
150 ml (¼ pint) rapeseed (canola) or sunflower **oil**
1 teaspoon **vanilla** extract
250 g (8 oz) peeled **carrots**, grated

Frosting (optional)
75 g (3 oz) low-fat vegetarian **cream cheese**
1 teaspoon **vanilla** extract
50 g (2 oz) **icing sugar**

To decorate (optional)
small pieces of **dried apricot**
mint sprigs

1 Put the flour, sugar, baking powder, cinnamon and nutmeg into a large bowl, stir to mix, then make a well in the centre. Stir in the eggs, oil, vanilla extract and carrots.

2 Line 10 sections of a 12-hole muffin tray with paper cases, and spoon the mixture into the cases. Bake in a preheated oven at 180°C (350°F) Gas Mark 4 for 25–30 minutes, until the muffins are well risen and golden brown. Cool on a wire rack.

3 Mix the frosting ingredients together in a bowl until smooth. Swirl a teaspoonful on top of each cake and decorate with the dried apricot and mint sprigs.

makes 10 **preparation time** 10 minutes **cooking time** 25-30 minutes

Index

Octopus Publishing Group Limited/front cover top right, front cover top centre, front cover centre, front cover centre left, front cover bottom centre, back cover top centre, back cover top right, back cover bottom left, back cover bottom centre, 3 top right, 3 centre right, 3 bottom right, 4 top left, 4 centre left, 4 bottom left, 5 top right, 5 centre right, 5 bottom right, 7 centre right, 8 top left, 8 centre left, 8 bottom left, 10, 13, 17, 20, 25, 30, 34, 38, 42, 49, 57, 60, 62, 64 /David Jordan front cover bottom left, back cover centre left, 2, 19, 28, 36, 46, 54, 58

Commissioning editor: **Nicola Hill**
Editor: **Abi Rowsell**
Senior designer: **Joanna Bennett**
Design: **Double Elephant/ Rita Wüthrich**
Production controller: **Jo Sim**
Picture researcher: **Jennifer Veall**
Proof reader: **Annie Lee**
Indexer: **Hilary Bird**